www.dinobibi.com

Author: Belinda Briggs
Editor: Kristy Elam
Illustrator: Jacqueline Cacho

CONTENTS

Native Plants & Animals (pg. 20)

Food, Culture & Traditions (pg. 24)

Famous People (pg. 37)

Major Cities & Attractions (pg. 40)

Bonjour! Je m'appelle Benoît Victor. My name sounds quite cool, non? Benoît is a common name for boys in France, although most of my friends just call me Ben. My middle name, Victor, is a family name; each generation has one boy with the name Victor. It's a tradition that started in the late 1800's. I have an ancestor from that time who loved Victor Hugo, the French novelist. I'm a big fan of Victor Hugo too. Sometimes when I meet people for the first time, I tell them that my first name is actually Victor.

Meet my Family

I have a big family, and a lot of my family members have cool names, too. I have two older brothers named Raphael (after the painter) and Gaspard (named after Gaspard Dughet, another painter). My big sister is named Antoinette, which is a very famous name is France, but she likes to be called Netty. You must think that my house is big and noisy with so many siblings, but actually it's just me, Mum, and Dad. Both of my parents have been married twice, and my siblings are much older than me; they're all in their twenties, and Netty is married and will be thirty next year!

Fun Fact
In France, the average family size is 2.3 people per household. This statistic is similar to those from other nearby countries such as Britain and Germany.

My Home, Saint-Malo

I live with my parents in Saint-Malo which is a port city in Brittany, in the northwest of France. It's a lovely place to live, but we don't spend our weekends here; we often travel to visit my siblings or my aunts and uncles. Yes, I've got a very big family indeed! Gaspard lives the closest to us; he lives in Dinan which is just across the bridge and only a 30-minute drive away. It's so close that sometimes he can come to our house for dinner. My other brother lives much further away. Raphael lives in Jargeau, which is quite close to Orléans, but that's a long way from us. Even further away is Netty; she lives in Calais. But it gives us an excuse to travel and see different places. As well as my three siblings, Dad has two brothers, and Mum has three sisters, so there's always someone to go and see!

The Saint-Pere beach and Solidor Tower in Saint-Malo, France

A French high speed train TGV, Anthéor, France

We often take the train when we go to visit family. Dad, who I call Papa, works as a train driver, so you'd think that he'd get sick of being on trains all the time. Actually, he loves it. He's never wanted to do anything else. Taking the train is popular because it's ecofriendlier than driving a car. Papa always likes to tell people about his job.

Religion in France

My Mum, who I call Maman, works in Saint-Malo. She runs her own business which is a little shop selling tourist items such as postcards, souvenirs, magnets, and locally made handicrafts. There's also a cold drinks fridge, and in the summer, she has a freezer selling icecream. She also runs a tour guide business in foreign languages. If people want a local tour guide to show them around the town, she offers the service in German and English. Mostly this is just in the summer, and someone else has to run the shop while she does the tour. Oh, and she also has a photograph service where she can take your photo and print it with the words 'Saint-Malo' at the top. My Maman is what you called a jack of all trades!

My parents aren't religious. Maman was brought up in a Christian family. If you ask her what she believes in, she usually shrugs her shoulders and says "Something... but I'm not sure what." My Papa is more certain — he doesn't believe in anything. Religion isn't a big part of French life, but we like to visit churches when we go to new places. Regardless of what the building is used for, the architecture is amazing.

School in France

When I was little, I went to a bilingual kindergarten so I could speak more than one language. When it was time for me to go to elementary school, I changed to a regular public school. Papa said I could speak English well enough to practice with Maman, and it would be better for me to be in a normal school. At first, I was sad because I had to make new friends in the public school. Actually, it all worked out for the best; many of my friends from kindergarten were the children of expat families who have since moved to other countries. So, we wouldn't have been together anyway! I quickly made friends in the elementary school. Papa was right; my English is still good without being in an international school.

Now I go to collège, which is French middle school. This school is where you go when you're 11 to 15 years old. After that is the lycée which is where you go until you are 18 years old. At that time, I will study for the baccalauréat. It's a French qualification which was introduced by Napoleon in the 1800's. If you want to go to university in France, you need to pass the baccalauréat.

Before we continue our trip, I would like to know more about you. Can you please complete this little questionnaire for me?

Your name:

Which country are you from:

Who are you traveling with?

Which places in France are you most excited about? Why?

St-Malo, Brittany, France

The Walls of Saint-Malo

We don't live in a big house. Actually, we just live in a small apartment. It sounds bad but it's actually a great place to live because of the location. Saint-Malo used to be a small port, but it expanded over the years. We live in the old city, which as the name suggests, is the oldest part of the town. Saint-Malo has new areas with bigger, newer houses in them. But outside of the old city things don't look as nice. The best part about our apartment is the location. Saint- Malo was a walled city, and the city walls still exist today. We have a top floor apartment and can look down on the city wall and the harbour. Beyond that, the view is of the sea!

Townhouses in Saint-Malo

Ramparts around Saint-Malo

Fun Fact

In French, the city walls are called les ramparts. Saint-Malo is not a big place, and it only takes about twenty minutes to walk all around the old city. Les ramparts are one of the most popular things for people to see in our town, and they're absolutely free.

Another free attraction is the lido, the outdoor swimming pool. Actually, the pool is on a beach, Plage de Bon Secours. In the summertime, I go to the beach almost every day of the week. France is big and has a lot of things to see, but Saint-Malo is my favourite place to be.

Fun Fact

In the summer, the population of Saint-Malo grows from around 50,000 to 200,000 people!

Plage de Bon Secours

Rivers of France

Remember I said that my brother Gaspard lived in Dinan? Dinan and Saint-Malo are separated by a river called the Rance. The river is over 100km long. The le Rance Tidal Power Station opened in 1966. It was the world's first tidal power station and is still one of the biggest in the world. While the Rance is important, it's certainly not the most well-known river in France.

Rance River along the town of Dinan

There are four major rivers in France: the Seine (777km/842 miles long), the Loire (1,012km/628 miles long, making it the longest river in France), the Garonne (602km/372 miles long), and the Rhône (813km/505 miles long). While the Rhône isn't the longest river in France, everybody knows it's one of the major rivers in Europe. It discharges twice as much water as the Loire, and it begins at the Rhône Glacier in the Swiss Alps.

Countryside Places

We have our own Alps too, called the French Alps, which have some magnificent mountains. But there are plenty of mountains which aren't just French; we share them with other countries. One example is Mont Blanc, which we share with Italy. It means 'White Mountain' and is a popular place for skiing and winter sports.

I've never been to the Alps. Papa doesn't like visiting cold places, and we don't have any family members living there. I've already told you that my brothers and sister all live in different places! One of Maman's sisters lives in Annecy. We've only been to visit my Aunt Delphine once or twice because Annecy is such a long way away. But Annecy is beautiful. Like Saint-Malo, it has an old town with traditional cobbled streets and a lovely river running through. Papa likes the architecture of the city, and we hired a boat on the Annecy Lake. I know it's a long way from us, but I'd like to visit her again. It was such a peaceful holiday. Maman's other sisters, Fleur and Anaïs, are twins. They live in Paimpol, so we see them much more often. Paimpol is in Brittany like Saint-Malo.

Mont Blanc literally means 'White Mountain' and is a popular place for skiing and winter sports. It is 4,808.7m (almost 3 miles) high.

Lake Annecy, Haute-Savoie region

Tourist Destinations

But these are all small, countryside places. I bet you're thinking, "Come on Benoît Victor. Tell us about some French places we've actually heard of!" Ok, I'll mention a few. Of course, you know all about Paris, right? It's one of the most famous tourist destinations in the world, so I don't think I need to say anything about that now, non? Bordeaux is a well-known place in France. Maman likes it because it's the wine capital of France, and there are so many delicious things to eat there. Mont Saint-Michel is another iconic place you've probably heard of. It's basically a town on an island and is one of the most visited places in Europe.

Something else about France you might like to know is the history of our flag. Our flag is called the Tricolour which means 'three colours.' Do you know what those colours are? Blue, white, and red. The tricolour design has become popular all over the world, and our flag is an important symbol of liberty. Have you seen a very famous painting called 'Liberty Leading the People' by Eugène Delacroix? The central figure is carrying the French flag above her head. If you go to Paris, you can see the painting in the Louvre.

WEATHER IN FRANCE

Bonjour mon ami, or hello my friend! I hope you are well and enjoying the day. Here in France, it's hot and sunny now. I love the summer weather just like my Papa does. But I also appreciate the change of the seasons and like to see the snow in winter.

Rhone River and Grand Colombier Bugey Alps Mountains

It doesn't snow every year in Saint-Malo because we're too far north. In the mountainous regions, it's always snowy, but I wouldn't like that either. A few days of snow a year is enough for me!

One thing we get a lot of in Saint-Malo is wind. That's because we live on the coast. When my Aunt Delphine came to visit a few years ago, she complained about the wind nonstop! She said that it gave her an ear-ache and she didn't know how we could bear to be battered about all year long. Maman laughed and said there was nothing wrong with the weather in Saint-Malo. "Good sea air — fill your lungs!" is what she always says when we walk along the ramparts on a windy day. Papa jokes that I have sea salt in my blood. When I was little, I used to want to be a fisherman so I could spend all my time rocking on the waves in my little boat. But of course, I was just a young kid then, and I've changed my mind many times!

Fun Fact
In Saint-Malo, the windiest months are during the winter, from November to February.

The Size of France

Something you mightn't realize about France is that it's big. The total area of France is more than 600,000 square km (248,573 square miles); that's twice as big as the United Kingdom. France is the 43rd-largest country in the world. Perhaps that doesn't sound impressive, but it's also the third largest country in Europe and the largest country in the European Union. We don't have the biggest population, though. We have a lot of space where there aren't very many people, like the mountain regions. Everyone thinks France is crowded because Paris is so popular, but it's actually a nice place to come and relax if you go to the countryside.

Pantheon, Paris

Sacre Coeur Cathedral, Paris

Our Temperatures

Because France is so big, the weather isn't the same across the country. Most of France has a temperate climate with a warm summer and plenty of rain. But then down in the south east of France, you get the extremes. Places with dry, hot summers and other places that are cold all year round. And of course, the mountains have snow all the time!

Paris is in central France and has average temperatures reaching 20°C (68°F) in the summer, and 5°C (41°F) in the winter. Bordeaux is on the Atlantic coast where it's wet and windy a lot of the time, and so temperatures are more like 16° C (60° F) in the summer, and 3° C (37° F) in the winter. The weather is colder in the east, in cities like Strasbourg which border Germany. There, it's 14° C (57° F) in the summer, and -2° C (28 °F) in the winter. Of course, the mountain areas are the coldest. Chamonix has average temperatures of 10° C (50°F) in the summer, and -6° C (21° F) in the winter. Brrr! If you like warm weather you should go to south France where it borders the Mediterranean. In Nice, the weather is 20° C (68° F) in the summer, and 5° C (41° F) in the winter.

Helping the Environment

Like everywhere in the world, the annual temperatures have been changing in France. Have you noticed that? It's because of climate change and global warming. I like having hotter summers because the summer isn't too hot to begin with in this part of France. But for hot countries the climate change means it's becoming unbearable. Something I'm proud of is that France is making a lot of big changes to help the planet. We care a lot about climate change, and that's because the government does, too. As Maman always says, change starts from the top down!

The French government officials have made a long-term plan about how to help the environment. You can tell that they really do mean it when they say they want to make a change. Afterall, the Rance Tidal Power Station was the first of its sort to open in the world. If France was thinking about renewable energy in the 1960's, you can believe that they're thinking about it now. Papa read me a report about what targets the government has set for the future. They want to achieve a 40% reduction in emissions by 2030 compared to 1990, and a 75% reduction by 2050. The year 2050 seems like it's a long way in the future, but I'm sure it will come around quickly. As we know, it doesn't take many years to damage the planet badly. So hopefully by 2050, we will have time to put some of it right.

Wind turbines

The government isn't just making big plans for the future. Things are happening all the time in France to make it a more eco-friendly country. In 2017, France opened the first ever solar-powered road. In 2016, it became illegal for supermarkets to throw away unsold food items. Now if there's food that's just out of date and can't be sold, the supermarket has to donate it. This is great news for the charities, food banks, and animal charities that get food for free.

What do you do to be more eco-friendly? I've been learning about how to save the planet at school, and my parents are also helping me learn about it. At home we always turn off the lights when we leave a room. Maman tells me not to waste time in the shower because it uses more water. When we cook something in the oven, we try to cook several things at the same time. This saves power and helps us to prepare meals in advance. It's fun finding ways to help the Earth!

Fun Fact

France has also imposed regulations on the fashion industry. Unsold textile items should be donated rather than burned.

15

In your country, are there any words or phrases that have significance? In France, 'revolution' is the most powerful word in our dictionary. "Vive la revolu tion" means 'long live the revolution,' and "Vive la France," means 'long live France.' We French are patriotic to our country, but in history we have also been loyal to various causes.

Vive la France

The phrase 'Vive la révolution' became well-known during the French Revolution. People didn't like the way the king was governing the country, so they rose up and overthrew the monarchy to create a republic. A few months after the revolution started, revolutionaries stormed the Bastille. The Bastille was an old fortress being used as a prison. When they stormed the Bastille, there were only seven prisoners inside. Everyone thought it was a waste of money to run such a big fortress for so few prisoners.

BATTLE OF WATERLOO (JUNE 18, 1815).

I have an interest in this period of history because of my name. I told you that my name is Benoît Victor, non? Well, the Victor part is after Victor Hugo who was a writer. One of his most famous books is *Les Misérables*, whiczh translates as 'The Miserables' in English, but people usually use the French name. I've heard that in English some people call it simply 'Les Mis.' This story was set in 1815 onwards. This date is important because it's just after the French Revolution. 1815 was the year that Napoleon lost the Battle of Waterloo.

Les Misérables

At its core, *Les Misérables* is all about revolution. The Revolution was about making changes that would make France a fairer place. The story focuses on many poor people who have terrible lives. If the rich people would share some of their wealth then life could be better for everyone. One of the most important themes is all about people trying to have better lives. One character is a poor, runaway convict who works hard to become a better person. He eventually becomes rich and adopts a little girl, who goes from being a poor peasant child to a well-off, well-educated young woman. *Les Misérables* is a work of fiction, but it's deeply rooted in French history. Fun Fact: Victor Hugo's *Les Misérables* has been turned into films, musicals, stage plays, and TV series. It's one of the longest running Broadway musicals of all time and over 70 million people have seen it.the French Revolution. 1815 was the year that Napoleon lost the Battle of Waterloo.

French writer, Victor Hugo

What do you know about Napoleon Bonaparte? He was the emperor of France from 1804 to 1814 and again in 1815 before he died. Many people consider him one of the greatest military leaders in the world. Did you know that he was born on an island, and died on another island? He was born in Corsica, which is a French Mediterranean island, in 1769.

Did you know?

Napoleon Bonaparte died on an island called Saint Helena, a British island on the west coast of Africa. He was exiled there by the British. They made him live in very bad conditions, and he died in 1821.

Napoleon Bonaparte

World War I and II

When people talk about French history, it usually has something to do with World War I or World War II. We've discussed these topics so many times in school. I know it's important to remember the wars, but sometimes I think we should study something else. People can get obsessed by things from history, can't they? My teachers love to talk about the world wars. I think that's because there's so much to talk about. The further you go back in history the less there is to say about it. That's because it's so far away from people who lived at that time. Go back far enough and there are no photographs or videos, no books written about it or diaries, just a few facts. But for recent history the material is endless!

First World War Memorial, Jougnes, France

World War I started off when archduke Franz Ferdinand was killed. Countries set up negotiations to try and solve the problems, and France was one of those countries. Some historians have said that the French wanted there to be a war. Others have said that the war was inevitable and not just because the French were pushing for it. The German government seemed very keen for a war, too. In the end, the Germans declared war on the French.

18 *French war monument in the village Aups in South France*

During the First World War, France suffered a lot. It wasn't long before they wanted the war to end. 1.3 million French people had been killed. Not only that, but a lot of land was ruined. Places where crops were grown couldn't be used anymore. the Paris Peace Conference was in 1919. Everybody was so shocked by what happened during the war that they wanted to make sure it didn't happen again. The different countries wanted to limit the power of aggressive countries like Germany. At the conference they also drew up new borders for countries.

But despite the hopes for peace, World War II started in 1939. The Germans invaded Poland, so France and Britain declared war on Germany.

United States Army WWII soldiers crossing a creek

Memorial and national cemetery containing remains of French and German soldiers who died on the battlefield at Verdun during the World War I.

The Germans acted quickly and invaded France. Quickly, the British troops were forced to flee France, and the country surrendered to Germany. But the French people didn't give up. Civilians set up resistance groups to fight against the Germans. The Second World War lasted event longer than the first one and had many more casualties across the globe. My grandpa was too young to fight in the war because he was just a boy, but his older brother went to war. He never came home. Grandpa never talks about it.

Wild Boar

My Little Goldfish

Do you have any pets? I've just been feeding my fish. He's a little goldfish named Flipper. On the day I brought him home from the pet store, he flipped right out of his fishbowl and onto the carpet. I had such a panic! After that we had to buy him a bigger tank. The new tank has a lid on the top so that if he jumps up, he won't fall out. Flipper is the colour of a tangerine and has big, buggy eyes.

I'd really like a cat or a dog but Papa says our apartment isn't big enough for that. Also, we like to go on vacation and visit our family all the time. It wouldn't be fair to make an animal travel all the time like that. When we go away, Flipper stays here by himself. We ask our neighbour to come in and feed him, but it doesn't take much work.

Marquenterre ornithological park, in the Nature Reserve of the Bay of Somme.

Small Animals in France

We don't have many pets in our house, but we do have a lot of plants and flowers. Maman loves to grown things, and she says having a lot of houseplants makes the air clean. We have a spider plant in almost every room in the house. Maman likes cacti, too. I think they're pretty when they have flowers on them. Some of Maman's cacti are covered in white fluff, and they don't look like plants at all. You have to be careful with cacti because it's easy to water them too much.

When people think of France, they don't usually think about the wildlife. People think about Paris, the Eiffel Tower, the Arc du Triomphe, baguettes, and croissants and pain au chocolat. But the natural world is important to French people, and the government has done a lot to protect it. It's easy to understand why we put so much effort into eco-friendly and energy efficient initiatives, like the solar powered road and the tidal power station.

I like going to nature reserves, don't you? Zoos are fun because you can see big animals like tigers and elephants, but they're not very nice. I wouldn't like being cooped up in an enclosure if I were used to roaming across a jungle or a plain. Maman doesn't agree with zoos; she thinks they're unethical. So, we rarely go to them. But nature reserves are different. At a reserve, the animals and insects have so much space to live in, and it doesn't feel man-made at all.

Fun Fact

The French government is committed to preserving natural spaces, and 10% of the country has been set aside for parklands and nature reserves.

Small animals are the best because you can easily get close to them. It's not recommended to get close to a lion! We have some native animals in France that are great fun to watch. The alpine marmot is one of my favourites because it has a lot of character. They live in mountainous areas in the south of France, so I've only seen an alpine marmot once in my life. The shrew, dormouse, mole, hare, and marbled newt are all much smaller than a rhino or other amazing zoo animal, but it's such a treat to see one. When you go to a nature reserve, it's like being a detective. You can't miss something as big as a giraffe, but if you're looking for a little newt you have to be slow and quiet and use your eyes.

Alpine Marmot, French Alps

Wild France

If you go into the wild, you never know what you're going to find. There are many places where you can go hiking and discover animals both big and small. Because France is quite big and has a lot of land that's still wild, the country can support a wide variety of animals. About 75% of the country is countryside. It's true! 25% of the country is completely wild forest. After that, about 50% is for farmland or other countryside which people are making use of, but it's still a good place for wildlife to live.

Papa and I like to go hiking in the forest with my brothers, although these days it's usually just me, Papa, and Gaspard. Raphael lives too far away. Sometimes we go camping too, but we have to make sure it's a safe place to camp. Usually, all we see are deer. However, there are other animals in the forests which could do us harm. Wild boar can be dangerous to people although they usually keep to themselves. They live in the lowland forests like the deer. But in the Alps and the Pyrenees, you get many more animals that are rare and exotic. Papa said he once saw a chamois antelope, which are quite rare. You can also see ibex, lynx, and brown bears, and of course the alpine hares.

Alpine Ibex, Aiguille Rouges

Into the Mountains

Down in the south on the Mediterranean coast-
line is a great place for bird watching. I'm not
such a fan of this, but Maman loves to watch the
wild birds. Some of them are migrating African
birds who aren't there all year round, like the
egrets, flamingos, bee-eaters, and vultures.

Across France, you get different plants in
difference regions because of the change in
climate and weather. In the Holarctic region,
which is more in the north, you get big, strong
trees like oak, beech, and pine. The plants that
grow here are hardy too; heath, juniper, and
lavender which smells amazing. In the northeast
you can see maple and larch. But down in the
Mediterranean side of France, different things
grow. The forests are full of sweet chestnuts and
fir trees. They also grow many citrus fruits like
orange trees.

Cevennes National Park

Bonjour, it's me again, Benoît Victor. Are you picking up any French phrases yet? French is a popular language to learn because, unlike other languages, it's spoken in more places than just the country it comes from. Naturellement, we speak French in France. But French is also the main, official language for 12 other countries. French is the official language for many countries in Africa, and it's also an official language in Canada. Countries that speak French include: Belgium, the Democratic Republic of the Congo, Haiti, Luxembourg, Madagascar, Rwanda and Switzerland. So, as you can see, French is a popular and useful language. Have you studied French in school before?

The Height of Sophistication

In France we have regional dialects, too. Dialects are sometimes close to the main language of the country they come from, but some are very different indeed. Breton is a French dialect which sounds nothing like French; it's more similar to Cornish or Welsh! Occitan is a dialect similar to French. But there's another language called Basque which is unrelated to any other language in the world. It's spoken is a small area between France and Spain. This sort of language is called an isolate. It's an isolated language because it doesn't have any genetic links to other natural languages.

Isn't it amazing that there are different languages in a country like France? What about in your country? Is your language popular or do very few people speak it? Whatever language your mother tongue is, I think it's important to study foreign languages. Maybe you will choose to study French? But even if you speak French, you might meet people in France who you can't understand because not everyone speaks our language!

La Bise

When you meet a French person, they won't give you a wave or shake your hand. Do you know how we greet each other in France? We kiss! This a tradition we call 'la bise,' is how we say hello to each other. La bise is different depending on who you are and your relationship to the person. For example, when my Papa meets his boss at work, they don't kiss. Also, if you don't know someone very well, then you're unlikely to kiss them. But if you're greeting friends of family, a peck on the cheek is the best way to say hello. Usually, la bise means two kisses; one on each cheek. But in some places in France they do four kisses! I think that's too many; one kiss on each cheek is enough for me.

French culture is famous all over the world. People think that the French are sophisticated, educated, forward-thinking, and creative. Also, people think the French are snooty and rude! This makes me laugh a lot because sometimes I can see that it's true. For example, if an American tourist is talking to a French waiter, it's easy to see how the American can get offended. But please, remember that this is just our way. We don't mean to be rude! We are very proud of France and our language, and this is why we might seem a bit rude to you.

French Fashion

I'm sure you know all about French fashion. Coco Chanel is one of the most famous in the world, along with Jean Paul Gaultier, Yves Saint Laurent, Christian Dior, Nina Ricci, and Louis Vuitton. I'm not interested in fashion, but I understand how France is the powerhouse of the fashion industry. Paris Fashion Week happens twice a year and is one of the most important events on the fashion calendar. If you ask me, sometimes those models look ridiculous. How can something be fashionable if it looks like it's falling to pieces? Sometimes they look like they're wearing something from the rubbish bin! Quelle folie! It's so crazy!

Don't be Rude

When you visit someone in your country, what do you take as a present for the host? In many countries it is customary to take a bottle of wine. But please, if you're invited to someone's house in France, don't let your parents bring a bottle of wine! In France, this is an offensive gift if someone has invited you for dinner. Of course, the host will have already chosen a nice bottle of wine. Their wine will be perfectly matched to go with the food.

If you bring a bottle as a gift, it means you think they can't choose a good wine by themselves! Perhaps a bunch of flowers will be better, non? Or chocolate? Everyone likes a box of chocolates!

Fun Fact

In France, children will often drink a small amount of wine with their dinner or on a special occasion. The French believe that, even for children, a little red wine is good for your health and that tasting alcohol when young helps children to learn to respect it.

A clock in Place De La Comedie. Central Bordeaux

Another thing to remember about visiting someone is that you shouldn't be on time. It's true! In many countries, if you are just one minute late the host will think its rude. But in France, if we invite you to arrive at 6:00 PM, we don't expect you until 6:15 PM. These extra minutes will give us time to prepare for your arrival, so don't be too early in France! But of course, this is just for someone's house. If you arrange to meet your friend at the cinema, don't be late or you could miss the film!

But perhaps you will spend time going to restaurants instead of visiting people's homes. Do you usually pick from a children's menu in a restaurant? In France, many restaurants don't have a menu just for the children. It always makes Papa laugh when we see a children's menu in other countries. He says "why do people think that children only want to eat fish fingers and chips, pizza and chips, or cheeseburger and chips?" Have you noticed that a children's menu doesn't have many interesting things on it? In France, adults believe children should try all different kinds of food. Children might not like everything, but if they have a chance to try it then they can learn about different tastes. If you can't find your usual favourites on a French menu, be brave and try something new!

Menu du Jour

Soupe à l'oignon

Cassoulet

Tarte Tatin

Yaourt Nature

Yaourt aux Fruits

Bon appétit!

Christmas in France

Do you ever get fed up when you're waiting for something? I know I do! My birthday was in the spring and Christmas is still ages and ages away! There's a new pair of running shoes I want but I won't get them for ages. When I'm older I'll get a part-time job, so I can buy what I want. At the moment, I have to wait for my birthday or for Christmas. I don't get pocket money any more. My grandma used to give me money for sweets when I was little, which I called bonbons. But now I'm older she thinks I don't need bonbon money!

I wonder if we celebrate Christmas like you do in your country. Some people call Father Christmas different names like Santa Claus, but we call him Père Noël in France. French people love cooking and eating. One of the best parts about Christmas is the feast! Do you eat a big meal on Christmas Day? We don't. In France, Réveillon is the name of the Christmas meal, and we usually eat it in the evening on Christmas Eve. Mmm, my stomach is rumbling as I think about it! Réveillon is one of the few times of year when my whole family is together, myself, my Maman and Papa, my brothers Gaspard and Raphael, and my sister Netty along with her husband. They all travel and visit us in Saint-Malo so we can eat the meal together.

Sometimes we have roast turkey or, if the aunts and uncles are visiting too, wehave a roast goose. Maman roasts the bird with chestnuts which become soft and sweet, almost like fudge. We have some vegetables, of course, but we also buy so much cheese and bread to eat with the roast bird. For pudding on Christmas Eve, we eat a chocolate yule log.

In Provence, which is a region in the southeast of France, they have a Christmas tradition that I'd really like to try. It's called the 'Thirteen Desserts.' These sweet treats represent Jesus and his twelve disciples at the last supper. First, there are the dried fruits and nuts which are called the 'four beggars.' There are figs, raisins, walnuts, and almonds. There are four types of fresh fruit, too. Usually you will have oranges, dates, grapes, melons, or pears. Now onto the good bit! You have sweets such as nougat, which is made with nuts and caramelized honey, or calissons, which is a sweet made from almond paste. Finally, the cake. Brioche is a sweet bread that traditionally should be torn by hand, not cut with a knife. There are also some sorts of pastries that are popular for the thirteen desserts too. It's made my mouth water just thinking about it!

Notre Dame De Paris at night

Bastille Day

Do you remember when I told you about the revolutionaries storming the Bastille? One of France's most important festivals is Bastille Day which happens on July 14th when we remember the storming of the Bastille. The historic event was the birth of French democracy, so it's still important to us today. There are military parades in big cities and smaller celebrations in towns and villages. Wherever you are in France on July 14th you can guarantee there'll be fireworks!

Fun Fact
Bastille Day is locally called "La Fête Nationale", which literally translates to "the national day".

Le Tour de France in 2013

Cycling Events in France

Have you heard of the Tour de France? It's another important event that happens in July. Cyclists from all over the world come to compete in this cycling event. The Tour de France has been going for over 100 years! The cycling route is different every year but includes the same breath-taking landmarks, such as the Alps and the Pyrenees. Also, the race always finishes down the Champs-Élysées, a very famous street in Paris. The race is split into stages. After each stage, the one who was the fastest gets to wear a yellow jersey, shows they are in the lead. After each stage, a new person gets the yellow jersey if his overall time was faster. On rare occasions, one cyclist wears the yellow jersey for the whole race! There are also other coloured jerseys for people who achieve other goals, like being a top cyclist under 25 years old or going very quickly on the mountains and hills! !

Professional cycling is a dangerous sport. On Mont Ventoux, there is a very steep hill, and one British competitor, Tom Simpson, had a heart attack there and died. Sometimes the spectators of the race or injured or killed too. Usually this happens when they're crossing the road. It's not just the cyclists, but also cars and vans with media supplies. There are always a lot of journalists, photographers, and TV crew people, so you need to be careful.

Fun Fact

The Tour deFrance was created in 1903 and the only time the race was cancelled was during the two world wars.

Local Festivals

Big festivals and events are fun, but I like the small ones, too. It's interesting to go to small places and see something unique. Do you remember that I told you my Maman's twin sisters Fleur and Anaïs live in Paimpol? The town only has about 7,000 people living there so it isn't big at all. However, Paimpol is in Brittany, so it's easy for us to visit. Anyway, what I wanted to tell you is this; Paimpol has a brilliant local festival. It's called the Festival du Chant de Marin, which means something like the 'sea shanty festival' or 'little wooden boat festival.' The little port fills up with wooden boats, and there is live music, too. A sea shanty is a song that sailors would sing on their boats. There are also traditional crafts and food stalls. The festival happens every few years and although most people haven't heard of it, I'd say it's unmissable!

Want to know about another local festival? It's called the Fête des Remparts and takes place in Dinan, where my brother Gaspard lives. It's a festival that will take you back in time to the Middle Ages. The festival has run once every two years since the 1980s and is a popular event. People dress up as knights in shining armour or maidens in fine dresses. One of the best bits is the jousting tournament, where the knights on horseback try to hit each other off their horses with a long stick. Everybody at the fair is wearing period costume, and you can visit the stalls to buy crafts and food.

If you're a movie buff then you've probably heard of the Cannes Film Festival. It was called the International Film Festival when it started more than 70 years ago, but in 2002 it changed its name to reflect the place where it's held. Cannes is on the French Riviera, which is a popular holiday destination throughout the year. At the festival, there are previews of films in many different genres. It's invitation only, and there are so many celebrities there. You can't go and see the films if you're not invited, but perhaps you'll see some celebrities on the red carpet. I'm not interested in watching it, but my sister Netty likes to see what outfits the celebrities wear to the event.

Fun Fact

The Cannes Film Festival is a hotspot for celebrity gossip and scandals that have nothing to do with the films!

My sister is interested in the movies, but like my brothers, I'm more interested in art. Because Gaspard and Raphael have artistic names, and I was named after a writer, we three have become more interested in art. Maman is quite creative and has always taken us to galleries and museums. I once went to the Paris Quartier d'été, which is a summer art festival in Paris. There are concerts, shows, circuses, performances, and other artistic events that take place over one month. The best thing is that many of the events at the Paris Summer Festival are free.

Jumbo circus facade design, Paris

Christmas market, Paris

Here in Saint-Malo, we have festivals too. Of course, there is always a big firework display on Bastille Day. In December, we have a Christmas market where there are so many good things to buy. I get such a warm, festival feeling at the Christmas market. Étonnants Voyageurs means 'amazing travelers' and is the name of a literature festival we have in Saint-Malo. Maman loves this because she's a real bookworm! Finally, Festival is a festival all about comic books and cartoons.

Fun Fact
Around 400 comic artists get together at the Quai des Bulles Festival in Saint-Malo.

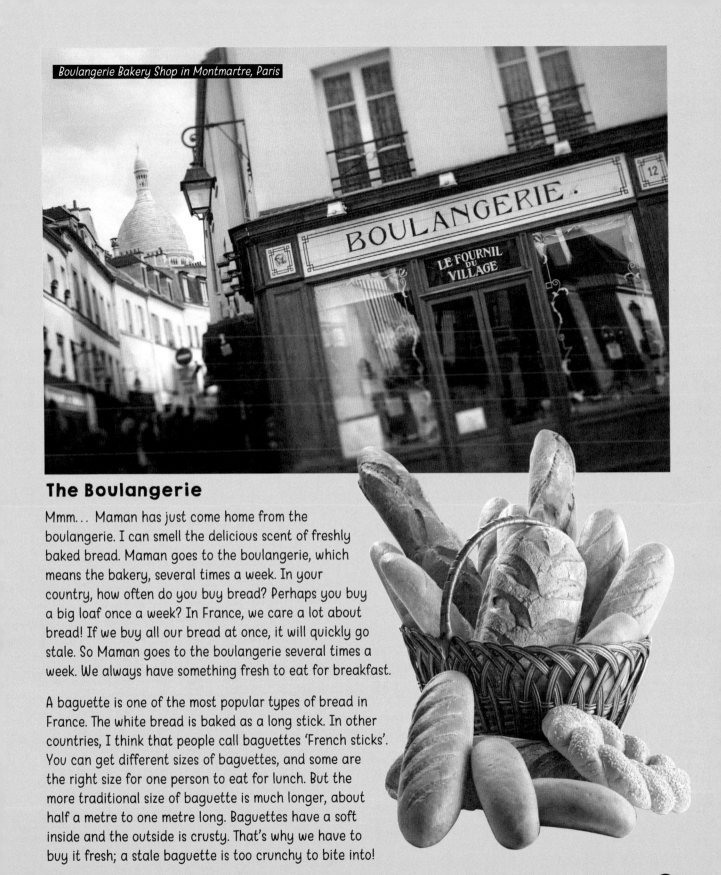

Boulangerie Bakery Shop in Montmartre, Paris

The Boulangerie

Mmm… Maman has just come home from the boulangerie. I can smell the delicious scent of freshly baked bread. Maman goes to the boulangerie, which means the bakery, several times a week. In your country, how often do you buy bread? Perhaps you buy a big loaf once a week? In France, we care a lot about bread! If we buy all our bread at once, it will quickly go stale. So Maman goes to the boulangerie several times a week. We always have something fresh to eat for breakfast.

A baguette is one of the most popular types of bread in France. The white bread is baked as a long stick. In other countries, I think that people call baguettes 'French sticks'. You can get different sizes of baguettes, and some are the right size for one person to eat for lunch. But the more traditional size of baguette is much longer, about half a metre to one metre long. Baguettes have a soft inside and the outside is crusty. That's why we have to buy it fresh; a stale baguette is too crunchy to bite into!

Sweet Treats

Something else Maman gets from the bakery are croissants. We don't eat croissants every day but usually just once a week. A weekend treat! That's because they're very buttery and have a lot of fat in them. Don't get me wrong, croissants are delicious! But I don't think it's good to eat them every day. There's another pasty I like called pain au chocolat, which some people call a chocolate croissant. That's silly because they look nothing like a croissant!

Fresh croissants with jam

Eclair with strawberries and cream shibust.

Another thing I like from the bakery are Éclairs. Have you ever tried one? The pastry is choux pastry which is filled with cream and topped with chocolate. Choux pastry isn't easy to make, so we always buy them from the bakery. They're absolutely delicious but not something you should eat for breakfast, of course. They're good for a treat or for a birthday. Papa likes Éclairs like I do, but Maman prefers to have an opera cake. This is a very rich, luxurious cake. It has thin layers of sponge that are soaked in coffee syrup and chocolateganache. It's too strong for me!

People in France really, really like bread. But these days we know that eating too much bread isn't good for you. It's important to eat a varied diet with a lot of fresh fruit and vegetables, as well as protein like meat or fish. In general, I'm not a fussy eater. I'll happily eat pretty much anything, even weird dishes. But my sister Netty is very fussy. She doesn't like meat or fish, and she doesn't eat much cheese either. All she wants to eat is bread! But I suppose it's fitting because of her name... I'll tell you about that later!

Unusual Meat

There are some French dishes that I like which I know foreigners aren't happy to try! One of these unusual dishes is escargots, which are snails. Escargot are land snails, not snails from the sea. Traditionally the snails are cooked in wine, garlic butter, or chicken stock. There's a special fork you can use to eat them. In France, snails are usually eaten as a hors d'oeuvre, which means a starter. I think they're delicious!

Escargot

Foie gras and cranberry chutney

Another delicacy is foie gras, which is the liver of a duck or goose. It's like pâté but much nicer because the geese or ducks are force-fed so that they get really fat. A lot of people don't want to eat foie gras because they think the animals are treated unkindly. Maman won't eat foie gras. I agree that perhaps it's not the nicest life for the animals, but then when I tried foie gras the taste was so incredible that I forgot about the unkindness. The taste is rich and smooth like butter and so delicate. Also, eating foie gras is part of our French tradition. People today might not agree with us, but it's an important part of our heritage. For a treat, Papa and I might choose foie gras in a restaurant. But of course, it's very expensive so I've only tried it two or three times in my life.

One thing I don't like are frog legs. We call them cuisses de grenouilles. I don't mind about eating frogs, but I just think its not worth the bother. I mean, they're tiny! Eating frog legs just seems like a waste of time to me. They don't taste like much, either. Papa likes them, and he likes cow tongue, too. In French, beef tongue is called langue de boeuf. That's not something I've tried, but Papa loves it. Papa is a real arnivore! Sometimes when we go to a restaurant, he orders steak tartare. That means a beef steak which is raw! Not cooked! It's chopped into little pieces and served in a lump. To me, it looks like cat food. I like meat, but I like it cooked first!

Crepes with Chocolate Sauce and Powdered Sugar

What will you try when you come to France? I bet you'll try eating crêpes because they're one of the most popular dishes for foreigners. I often see people walking around Saint-Malo with a chocolate filled crêpe. They're nice, but I recommend you try a galette. That's a savoury pancake with brown flour and you can have it for lunch. My favourite comes with ham and egg. A cheese galette is nice too. Hmm, what else? Many foreigners like to try French mussels. The best dish is Moules-frites. This is a bowl of mussels served with chips, which I think are called French fries when you go abroad.

Oh, got to go! Maman is calling me for breakfast. It's not baguette or croissants we're having today… it's beignet. I like these pastries because the sound like my name. My favorite is beignet pomme, which means it has an apple sauce filling. You can also get beignet filled with chocolate, custard, raspberry, banana, peach… delicious!

Maria Antonia

Do you remember that I said I'd tell you why it's funny my sister Netty likes bread so much? It's a long story. In 1755, a princess was born in Austria. Her name was Maria Antonia, and she was one of sixteen children, although not all of them survived. When she was fourteen years old, Maria Antonia got married. Actually, at the first ceremony, her husband wasn't even there. She was married by proxy and hadn't even met him yet! She met her husband for the first time in a forest. Her husband was Louis XVI of France, so she became Queen of France. At this time, she changed her name to the French version, Marie Antionette. Some people liked her a lot because she was young and beautiful. But she was Austrian and not French, so some people didn't like her very much.

Did you know?

Marie Antionette was 37 years old when she died. She was executed for treason and was the last Queen of France before the French Revolution .

Queen Marie Antionette and King Louis XVI were married in 1770, but they didn't have a baby until 1777, which was another reason people didn't like her. Marie Antionette made changes at court, too. She stopped wearing the traditional heavy make-up and fancy dresses that court women wore. She wanted to wear a simple muslin dress instead, but people complained. They said the queen should wear something fancy not something simple. Marie Antionette had a difficult time as queen, and it only got worse as she grew older. She had four children, but only one survived into adulthood.

As you might have guessed, my sister Netty has the same name as the Queen; her full name is Antionette. Remember I said that Netty loves to eat bread and cake? Well, one of the most famous stories about Queen Marie Antionette is about cake, too. There was a time when the peasants in France were starving and didn't have any bread to eat. Someone asked the queen what they should do about it. The queen was living a luxurious life, so her answer wasn't very serious. When she heard that the people had no bread, she said "let them eat cake!" But actually, historians say that there is no evidence Marie Antionette said this. Isn't history fascinating?

I think I told you that it's not just my sister who has a famous name, non? My big brothers have well-known names, too. Gaspard is the brother who lives nearby in Dinan. He's named after the painter Gaspard Dughet. The painter was actually born in Rome and was half French, half Italian. Sometimes the painter is called Gaspard Poussin because his tutor was a man called Nicolas Poussin. He was a painter in the 1600s, and his work, mostly landscapes and classical Roman scenes, was popular with British art collectors. My brother Raphael is also named after a painter. The painter Raphael was actually Italian. He lived in the 1400s and painted several religious scenes. But Raphael is a popular name in France as well as Italy.

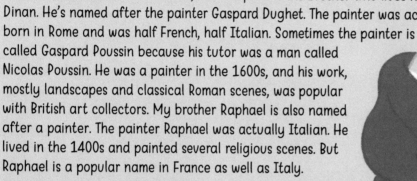

Victor Hugo: Exiled

As I've told you, I was named after a famous French writer. Victor Hugo lived in the 1800s and is most famous for his work *Les Misérables*. He had political views that not everyone agreed with. He was exiled from France and had to move to different places. Eventually he went to the island of Guernsey in the Channel Islands. Guernsey is easy to travel to from Saint-Malo; you can get the boat directly. He lived on the island for around 15 years before he was allowed to return to France.

Victor Hugo's books have a lot of sad things in them. I think Victor Hugo led quite a sad life and experienced many difficult things. His first child died as a baby. He had four more children, but there was more sadness waiting for him. His eldest daughter and favourite child died when she was 19 years old. It was her wedding day, and she was on a boat. When the boat overturned, her heavy dress got soaked with water, and she drowned. Her young husband also drowned as he tried to save her. This must have been terrible news for Victor Hugo. He found out about his daughter's death by reading it in the newspaper. He had another daughter who had a severe mental illness and lived in an insane asylum for some time. He also had a son who died in his forties from an illness, and his other son died before he him as well. Poor Victor Hugo!

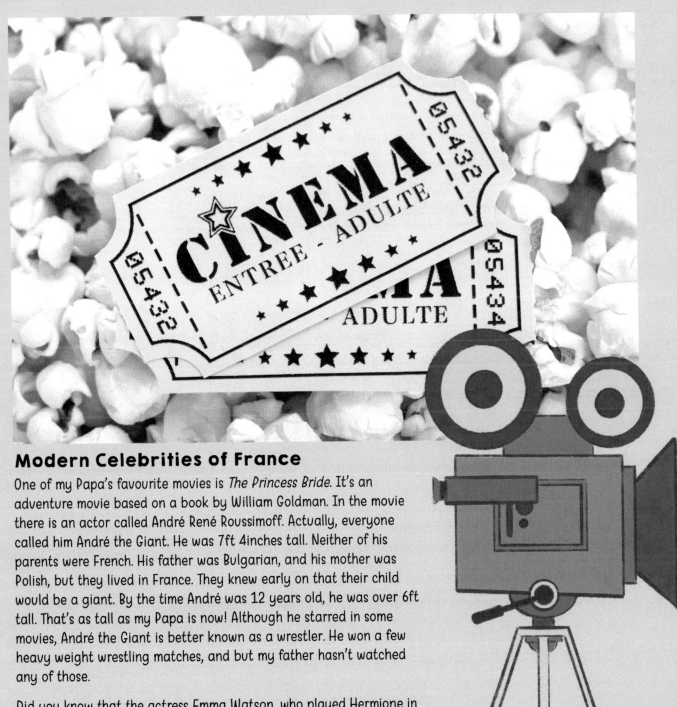

Modern Celebrities of France

One of my Papa's favourite movies is *The Princess Bride*. It's an adventure movie based on a book by William Goldman. In the movie there is an actor called André René Roussimoff. Actually, everyone called him André the Giant. He was 7ft 4inches tall. Neither of his parents were French. His father was Bulgarian, and his mother was Polish, but they lived in France. They knew early on that their child would be a giant. By the time André was 12 years old, he was over 6ft tall. That's as tall as my Papa is now! Although he starred in some movies, André the Giant is better known as a wrestler. He won a few heavy weight wrestling matches, and but my father hasn't watched any of those.

Did you know that the actress Emma Watson, who played Hermione in *Harry Potter*, was born in France? She doesn't have a French family but her parents were living in Paris when shze was born. And do you know the actor Johnny Depp? His wife was French and their daughter, Lily-Rose, was born in France. The film director Roman Polanski has a Polish name, but he, too, was born in France. My country is a popular place for people to live in, and so many people who have family from different places are actually born in France.

It's a Mystery

Don't you just love a mystery? I used to love detective novels when I was a kid. These days I read mystery novels for older kids, but you can't beat a real-life mystery. Papa just read me something from the newspaper which sounds like it's straight out of a detective novel. Two or three hours from Saint-Malo, there is a coastal town called Plougastel Daoulas. I've been once or twice before, and the town has hit the headlines recently over a mysterious stone.

Vintage engraving of a Fishing Boat of Plougastel, Brittany 19th Century

The rock has some unusual carvings on it, and no-one can understand them. As well as the indecipherable words there are some pictograms too, such as a heart, a boat, and a cross. The dates 1786 and 1787 appear on the rock; these are the dates that the Fort du Corbeau was built. Also, in 1920, a Russian solider added the date to the rock. But the original message is still unknown. Isn't it fascinating? I believe the local community is running a competition to see if any linguists can work it out. Next time I visit Plougastel-Daoulas, I definitely want to visit that rock!

But I don't think I'll get to visit any time soon. Maman wants our next trip to be to Lourdes, a town in the foothills of the Pyrenees. She went there once when she was a girl. Papa is happy to go because he can enjoy walking in the mountains there. But for most people, a visit to Lourdes is a pilgrimage. Christians come from all over the world to see the grotto which has special water. It's said that the water from the spring has natural healing properties. Sometimes a very sick person drinks or bathes in the water, and they suddenly get well, like a miracle. The church has recognized around 70 miraculous healings, and so many sick people go there because they hope to be cured too. But of course, 70 is a very small number out of the hundreds of thousands who visit!

Did you know?

Pougasted-Daoulas is also famous for their strawberries known as gariguette de Plougastel!

Basilique du Rosaire and Supérieure in Lourdes

A Miracle at Lourdes

One of the best-known facts about Lourdes is about the Virgin Mary. In 1858, a young girl called Bernadette Soubirous was at the grotto when she saw Mary, the mother of Jesus Christ. The apparition appeared to the girl many times and asked for a religious sanctuary to be built for her there. They called her Our Lady of Lourdes. While not everyone believed Bernadette, eventually the church agreed with her story. After she died, Bernadette was sainted. Her body was exhumed several times after her death and many decades later. The fact that her body still looked fresh and hadn't corrupted made people believe how holy she was.

So Many Castles

Raphael and his girlfriend recently went on holiday to Dordogne. They sent us a lovely postcard. I've never been there before, but it looks like a great place. It's a top location to visit if you like castles; there are over 1,500 castles in Dordogne. The Château de Rocamadour sits on top of a hill and looks like it could easily fall off. The view from the top must be incredible and you can watch a falconry display, too. Château de Castelnaud is a mediaeval castle, and Raphael said it has an amazing collection of weapons. The military history tour can give you so much information about this place. To visit Château de Val you need to get on a boat, and Château de Castelnau-Bretenoux has six towers to enjoy the views from. There are so many castles I want to visit in Dordogne!

Fort La Latte, France

Papa and I love to visit castles. But we don't need to go all the way to Dordogne to see them. In Brittany, where I live, there are plenty of places to visit. Fort La Latte is a nearby castle I've been to. It's right on the edge of a cliff and can be very windy! It's not a big castle, but I enjoy standing on the old stones and looking out to sea. Josselin is another castle in Brittany which is very pretty. It has tall towers with spires that look like upside-down icecream cones. Do you like visiting castles in different countries?

Raphael travels a lot and has been to so many amazing places. Last year he went to Carcassonne which is also famous for its castle. It's a UNESCO world heritage site and dates back to Roman times. The town also has an amazing bridge which looks brilliant at night time. The bridge has lights underneath which sparkle on the water. I'd love to go to Carcassonne, but maybe not in the summer. The hottest August temperature for the town was over 40 degrees Celsius!

Medieval town of Carcassonne

Mont saint Michel - Normandy, France

Eiffel Tower, Paris

Have you heard of Mont Saint-Michel? Perhaps I told you about it before. Mont Saint-Michel is an island in Normandy, and only 50 people live there most of the time. There are fortifications on the rocky island which make it look like the whole place is a castle. It's fun to visit; you get there by walking over the causeway. But you have to pay attention to the ocean. If the tide comes in before you've walked back, you'll be stuck! Walking down the narrow-cobbled streets is like stepping back in time. It was a favourite place of the French composer Claude Debussy. I'm amazed that there haven't been any movies filmed on the island because it's completely picturesque.

Paris isn't Perfect

Paris, of course, is a place you must visit. But be warned; it might not be everything you're expecting. Have you heard of Paris syndrome? It's when tourists go to Paris, and they suffer extreme shock because Paris is so different than what they expected. Sometimes the tourists need to fly home with a doctor because they're so upset! It sounds like a crazy new illness but the first doctor to talk about it was in the 1980s. Usually, Japanese visitors suffer from Paris syndrome. They have the idea that Paris will be a very pleasant, romantic, amazing place. But like any city, Paris isn't perfect! Usually there are about twenty Japanese people who suffer from this every year, and they are often young women who have never traveled abroad before. But don't worry; most visitors to France don't suffer from this sort of culture shock!

Notre Dame de la Garde in Marseille

Ça, alors! There are so many other places I want to tell you about! Marseille has a population of over 800,000 people and is the second largest city in France. You should visit the church near the station there. Also, eat the bouillabaisse; it's a delicious fish stew. Lyon was the capital of France in Roman times. Visit the Fourvière Hill for amazing views across the city. If you're interested in movies, when you're in Lyon you should go to the Musée Miniature et Cinéma.

Basilica Notre Dame de Fourviere

Do you like Dijon mustard? How about a trip to Dijon? When you go, try to visit somewhere with a great view so that you can see the pretty rooftiles. Finally, Strasbourg is on the border with Germany and is such a cool place to visit. It's the blending of two cultures, French and German. Christmastime is the best time to visit because of the market they have. It's the greatest place for Christmas shopping!

CONCLUSION

C'est pas possible! I can't believe we have come to the end of our time together. Oh la la. Well, I hope I've taught you many interesting things about France along the way. It's not just baguettes and the Eiffel Tower, non? France is such a varied place. Whatever you want to do, I'm sure you can do it in France. Shopping, sightseeing, country walks, sports, fine dining... there is everything and anything you can imagine.

We French people mightn't always seem so friendly, especially in big cities. But remember that we are a proud people with big hearts. You just need to get to know us! France is full of foreigners, both tourists who visit time and time again, and those who come and never want to leave! Perhaps you'll be one of those people, non? Well, I hope you enjoy France! Bonne chance!

Which parts of France did you like the most and why?

_____

_____

_____

_____

_____

_____

What activities did you enjoy most and why?

_____

_____

_____

_____

_____

_____

Now, to our pop quiz! Good luck!

Which region of France is Saint-Malo located in?
a) Corsica
b) Normandy
c) Brittany

(answer (c) — Brittany)

In Saint-Malo, which is in Brittany, what is the average summer temperature?
a) 7°C
b) 18°C
c) 24°C

(answer (b) — 18°C)

After Paris, which tourist destination in France has the most hotel rooms for visitors?
a) Lourdes
b) Lyon
c) Marseille

(answer (a) — Lourdes)

You can spot wild lynx in the French mountainous areas, but what is a lynx?
a) A bird
b) A wild cat
c) An insect

(answer (b) — A wild cat)

What percentage of the European Union speak French?
a) 5%
b) 8%
c) 12%

(answer (c) — 12%)

Which of these is the biggest city in France?
a) Paris
b) Lille
c) Nice

(answer (a) — Paris)

What are the dates of World War II?
a) 1939-1945
b) 1935-1939
c) 1938-1944

(answer (a) — 1939-1945)

Which French festival is held in May?

a) Lemon festival
b) Paris Autumn festival
c) Neighbours Day

(answer (c) Neighbours Day)

Which of these French cities has the smallest population?
a) Marseille
b) Lille
c) Toulouse

(answer (a) — Marseille)

When was the first Tour de France cycling competition?
a) 1903
b) 1910
c) 1918

(answer (a) — 1903)

Feel free to visit us at www.dinobibi.com and check out our other titles!

Dinobibi Travel for Kids

Dinobibi History for Kids

 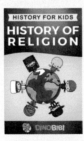 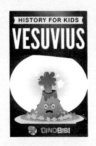  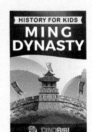

Made in the USA
Middletown, DE
07 December 2021

54470249R00027